A new look at Autism and Dementia

(a personal exploration)

(October 2015)

*

research essay

(first draught)

*

Traumear

Paperback ISBN 978-1-7948-9562-1

*

www.traumear.com

Autism and Dementia etc.

Initial considerations and points to ponder:

- That the so-called 'symptoms' are transferred, from the normal to the afflicted person.
- That the potential of wholeness exists in afflicted persons; hence the symptoms of persecution-type in so-called normal (modern) individuals.
- That the modern individual is dual with delusory social overlay, through which the afflicted person readily sees and which is interpreted as betrayal. Hence the perceived need, by the 'normal' individual, for protection of his supposed (but lacking) wholeness.
- Can 'autistic' persons be usefully considered to have 'soul' in a soulless social environment? (vide: G. Jung's title: Modern Man in Search of a Soul)
- An 'autistic' person should not be viewed in isolation nor merely in society but also in communal relation. Otherwise the contradiction of soul versus lack of soul speaks too loudly.
- That a modern, divided-in-himself individual may seek to be, expect to be, 'healed' by caring for an 'autistic' or 'demented' person.
- A better, more accurate term, instead of 'autistic', which seems to accentuate self, when in fact self is precisely and painfully absent – self (take note!) as insistence on duality as a right by the social individual – might be **unique**. So here we actually have the prime example of the modern professional who comes up with the term 'autistic' to describe his own self-possession (possession by self) which he has transferred to the unique one. (The social individual insists on his right to be modern-

dualistic, i.e. always and at any time at liberty to observe himself as it were correctly, rightly.)

- So: not 'autistic' but unique?
- The 'show' of the unique one is both defence against the dualism of the social individual, which is correctly felt as false and threatening, and is also healing-behaviour during periods of rest.
- 'Wilfulness', 'obstinacy' have to be looked at generously in the special case of the 'blessed, unique person'.
- Not autistic but blessed – this term too, like unique, stripped of sentimentality.
- Blessed, gifted – (also 'savant'?) The so-called 'savant' characteristics also need to be seen as protection-devices, defence mechanisms.
- Ask: What can we, who are supposedly normal and not afflicted in this way, gain from the introduction of these unique, blessed persons into our midst? Is this introduction to be regretted by us or to be considered as providential?
- Lay aside the supposition that you are well while they are ill. Think rather that they have what you miss, what can be of benefit for you – mostly in terms of wholeness.
- Unconditional love as affective communication. One cannot expect unconditional love from social individuals, who may be materialistic, legalistic, rights-conscious. So in their case one would counsel an **honourable approach**. Let them be mindful of what they stand to gain by honouring the unique person.

* *

What about 'new body' as the gift itself, rather than 'soul'. {New body as vision (sight, hearing touch etc.), emotion rather than emotions, passion rather than passions, certainties rather than opinions; even thought rather than thoughts, especially in the case of dementia.}

The social individual misses emotions in the one endowed with 'new body' emotion; misses passions in the one endowed with 'passion'; same with vision, senses etc. He wants to arouse emotions, passions, sympathies, i.e. social signs, whereas the new body is, and shows no signs. This lack of signs is probably worth looking at closely. The 'pearl of great price' is rejected by the modern social individual because it looks like nothing else, reminds of nothing with which he is familiar.

The unique, blessed person is helped if he is allowed and encouraged to be, rather than to do, by those who wish to benefit from him –The new body as soul operation? [1]

Why unique *person*, when precisely personality seems so absent? when 'communication skills' seem so awry?

Perhaps what we have here are negative, or affective attempts at communication; in other words, semiconscious expressions of pain, affliction, hardship. The communication is affective, thus coincidentally highlighting the lack of human-natural affection in the social individual.

Another, more elaborate take on this aspect of our topic: The gifted one (autism, dementia) does not understand that he is gifted or how he is gifted, but is drawn in that direction, affectively. If he were left to his own devices completely he would not arrive at any rationality, because after all the giftedness is potentially communal, not isolated, merely individual. Not only that, but the only sign to alert others would, as a consequence, be negative, a lack of expression, of recognizable being and doing. A total lack of external challenge is hypothetical, not very likely, since, one assumes, there would al-

---

[1] See the author's essay: The New Body.

ways be some reminder to 'come out of oneself', even if merely survival were at stake (hunger and thirst, cold, risk to life and limb). The carnal effects would play at least some subsidiary role (vide: feral children, street children).

For our purpose, the influences on the unique one that interest us are 1. those that are Social – lay (the public attitude) and professional (psychiatrists etc.) – and 2. those that are communal, considerate, merciful.

A propos 'affection': This is a crucial point, in my opinion. Observe first of all the lack of human-natural affection, of childlike intimacy, in the social individuals, who need to guard themselves against any discovery of their more or less chronic (modern) duality of nature and spirit. So the unique one is *affective* in the sense of: "Look, this is what I am like, this is who I am, let me show you, so that you might help me. If you refuse to help me or cannot help me, I am bound to get angry, even furious; even self-harming and self-destructive, (or in the opposite direction, resentful, moody, bitter?) because I sense that deep down you seek to be rid of me. (Do we not also look in vain for signs of affectation in the unique one? Of ego?)

Surely we do well always to distinguish, in ourselves, between the social individual and the communal person. Always decide/opt for the latter. Communicate at least through being.

*

Wrong to think of the 'autistic' one as abnormal in an allegedly 'normal social environment'. The 'modern' individual is divided in himself, fearfully or arrogantly conscious of this but not aware. Consequently he comes up with social defence-and-attack behaviour, mechanistic (egotistic) to a degree, especially when affected by someone he thinks of as the abnormal, 'autistic one', whom he cannot comprehend, because here no dualism needs to be confronted but duality is being erased, replaced, by soul/new body as potential oneness.

The modern divided individual, who is not really personal because his social presence is a false unity, which means that communication cannot properly work for him – this individual might be able to respond to a so-called spirit healer (Tolle, Krishnamurti etc.) who ignores his duality while introducing him to the possibility of soul-awareness. The 'autistic', unique one, by comparison, coincidentally (not intentionally) has the effect of bringing to the attention of the social, modern individual, perhaps even forcefully, that individual's soul-deficiency, very likely experienced by the unique one as duplicity and betrayal.

Also, I suspect that the 'unique one' would secretly like to be 'found out', that is to say, he would quite human-naturally prefer that his potential oneness (soul/body) be recognized. This may be a less than conscious wish of his. Consequently *some of his behaviour* might be interpreted correctly in that direction. Think of him as in prison, (Mt. 25:36, 43) hoping to be visited. Other behaviour might be interpreted in terms of protection against abuse and perceived torture, and thirdly in terms of authentic insistence on uniqueness (new body), readily misinterpreted as badness by social individuals.)

So three strains of behaviour: 1. appealing, 2. protective, 3. authoritative. While we look for these, we are less likely to make social or clinical judgments, which close the door to any understanding and to any mutual healing progress.

The overall approach of the *friendly helper* however is always unconditional love, due to which any prejudice in himself is bypassed. All the same, since so many different kinds of behaviour and lack of behaviour seem to turn up in these unique ones, why not keep one's eyes open for an exaggerated presence of one of these three strains: The 'savant' characteristic, for example, might beneficially be seen as authoritative uniqueness. The avoidance of eye contact points to the protective strain, while the lining up and ordering of a multitude of objects might make sense as an appeal. This is information for *us* and we do not draw his attention to it, as if to stop him from doing it.

The modern individual – call him simply the individual or perhaps the social individual, who cannot, for that reason be truly personal – is alerted, due to the 'autistic' or 'demented' one in his presence, to his insufficiency, to the sham of his societal, non-communal being and he reacts in any number of ways, and these reactions, essentially fearful, are accidentally picked up by – unfortunately transferred to – the unique one. They account for his so-called symptoms. He has to defend his oneness against the rawness, the egotism, the modern duality of the social individual.

Remember that the oneness of the unique one is initially only potential, however nonetheless present to him as what we might think of as a hidden treasure to which he senses himself to be biologically/spiritually contracted. His struggle against interference is only conscious, not yet aware. We do well never to ignore that these unique ones are placed in our midst for our benefit, to alert us to the shortfall of our modernity and all that that entails. So in that sense we might start by helping ourselves rather than trying to help them, and punishing them when we fail.

So we do well to keep in mind that we as modern individuals are as much in need of help as these 'unique ones'. We need to be able to let go of our individualism, confirmed and hardened as it may still be due to our trust in society as a workable end in itself. We mistake this individualism, on which we frequently insist, for personality, and from the spurious vantage point of this pretend-personality we judge what we call the lack of personality of the unique one. The confusion is appreciable. If we hope to make progress, we can profitably begin by looking honestly at what disturbs us about the unique one. As soon as we sincerely and in earnest reflect on the elemental varieties of shame and terror, guilt and horror, however minimal, of which we are hopefully still capable, we begins to make progress out of our individualism towards soul/new body and true personality.

The help the unique one needs is recognition of his incumbent soul and of the incumbency of his soul/new body (weighing him down, burdening him, especially to the degree that he finds no communicant).

To what shall we compare the incumbent soul under harsh societal treatment? To a tortured person, perhaps? In prison and tortured?

Imagine alone this, that you are the only one among many, who realizes what it means to be without that god-given unifying principle, inasmuch as you are daily exposed to soulless creatures, while you yourself cannot find recognition for the soul you at least dimly believe you have.

That there is no directly identifiable correlation between the unique one's uncommon behaviour and the behaviour of those near him, should not surprise us because we social individuals do, after all, practice concealment of our guilty and shameful self-alienated condition behind a more or less painstaking construct of appearances that are to adapt us to this thing called society; (which is, of course a thing, not a being, only insofar as it is perceived as a final, or finally realizable, state).

Any merely social behaviour must be 'felt' by the one with 'new body' as terrible and horrible. No wonder that he terrifies and horrifies, in his turn then, the social individual, saying to him – shouting it perhaps – "You are not whole and yet you behave towards me as though you demanded I should be like you."

Any mutually salvific process, in the absence of a ready friend – of someone who understands – would then depend on some social individual becoming truly friendly – i.e. admitting that he has much to gain from association – of the exploratory, communal kind – with the unique one.

Why is it to be expected that a child with a secret, still undamaged soul/body, is not very likely to risk, except in an alarming way – the security afforded by it?

The child fears ‘the revelation of the secret the depth of which lies hidden from his own eye.’

Search in the child’s eyes for the revelation of that secret.

*

The unique one, in an environment of normal society – there is pressure to be social, to be not unique.

What needs to be learned by the unique one is how to blend in without loss of uniqueness. In a similar way, we not social but communal beings blend in too by saying certain words, such as: ‘Hello, good morning, how are you?’ If someone says: ‘How are you?’ we do not tell him how we are, because that would shock this social individual and he might become unpleasant. We don’t want that. What would we gain from shocking someone? So we say: ‘Fine. I am fine, thank you for asking.’ Social behaviour is like this. We who are communal gladly bow to the pressure of correct social rules and to behaviour according to those rules. Does that mean we lose our unique soul? Not if we are careful. If we wish to walk through the high grass where adders may be sunning themselves, quite innocently, we might not say: Very well, I will not go through that meadow. Nor do we stamp on ahead in our bare feet in righteous anger at adders but – we wear boots. This decision, this art, of being careful among those who are not unique, who have no soul and exist as well as they can according to the rules of their society – like this in Burma, like that in Finland – can be learned. However a social individual cannot teach this care, as must be obvious. At best he may shun or criticize us, for doing ‘what is not done!’. The adder knows only adder existence. Should we blame it for biting a bare foot that steps on it? The *friend*, a whole human being, a unique, individual person, can teach it. Experience and pain are also good teachers.

Goethe, in some of his early poems, imagined himself a blundering bear in the patrician society during his early manhood. Soon enough he found out who the real bears were and he learned to be careful. Genius is exceptionally unique; especially unique. We may suppose we are plagued by genius because our genuine thought gets us into trouble in the society shocked by our outspokenness. Should we keep our mouth shut altogether, we 'autistic', unique ones? That seems safe at times and sometimes that is the best we can do. Remain silent. (Consider genius too as uniqueness mistaken for egotism.) Someone present manages to make a helpful comment. A true friend helps us out of a tight spot. We were stuck, fixated in ourselves. Perhaps we are very poor in spirit. We are literally frightened to death sometimes, among people – in the society of people. What is it that worries us? We stutter. We are silent again but our breast feels so constricted, we feel we might explode. A rage builds in us. Perhaps we will rush out of the room. Not that we necessarily blame someone, hold someone responsible, for the soul-pain we feel (without suffering it) but we do feel this dreadful panic, embarrassment, anger, you name it. (I wonder does anyone ever weep in such an awkward situation? Perhaps that is never the case.)

We notice also how social individuals appear to lead healthy and happy lives. They may be good performers, illusionists, actors. A momentum has to be kept up or the cracks will show.

Can we learn to identify particular occasions where friendly help is needed, without generalising and saying: All those who behave like this can be helped? Is a theory required?

Let us instead remain open and alert to the next time when a friend is needed and we might be it – because we have previously – and perhaps often – thought about how one might be helpful to an 'autistic', unique one. Perhaps we have learned already, from our befriending of such a unique one, how we might in similar fashion help someone who is socially inept and in the prison of his repressed/indolent soul – called psyche.

*

Psyche is the prison. The soul is the freedom.

We may simply use the word soul to denote a human being's freedom. Psyche, then stands for that state of incarceration where nothing is possible and there is no hope.

A soulless, or psychic, individual may nonetheless be observed to be active and passive, except that when we wish to communicate with him we come up against a massive hindrance that prevents communication. The hindrance to true communication may be slight or seemingly total, however the character of the hindrance is always massive. (incapable of form or shape)

We are bound to find this most disturbing when our offer of communication is not accepted. Of course we may try to overcome what we take for a partial rejection of our offer, and the way this is done is bound to differ from one time to the next and from one individual to the next. Meanwhile we maintain our own freedom. We are no use to anyone if we ourselves become 'imprisoned' in psyche – and there is always that risk. What minimizes the risk is that our humanity is kept clear of prejudice. – The professional approach, by comparison, is not clear but inhibited by misleading suppositions that actually confirm the psychic state of the massively inhibited individual.

*

On one hand, we should not expect to be able to discuss, beneficially, his psychic state with an inhibited individual. He is 'imprisoned' precisely in the sense that he actively hides from his awareness any psychic involvement. This barrier cannot be broken down by anyone, not by the impaired individual because he precisely depends on it for his security from further disturbance, nor by a well-meaning helper with the aid of logic or reason or even forceful good sense, because it is the very character of psychic impairment that nothing from without, nothing that can be experienced, is to be trusted. It makes no sense therefore to try to impress upon the handicapped individual that he is responsible for his deplorable condition and that he should make an effort to co-operate with a prospective helper to improve himself.

So what about that barrier? There is none for the human being, for the prospective and hopeful helper. He faces for the moment the truly impossible. On what level can he possibly – in power – make contact with this prisoner of fate?

Why, he knows it even now. He cannot help but god will help.

(So well then, let god help. Nothing to do with me. I go home and tend to my chickens.)

Ah, but wait a moment. Imagine that god cannot do it without you. God is spirit and here human being is at stake. Would you please consider that god within you requires no enchantment but your soulful cooperation, if anything is to be achieved?

Oh very well. Let him win me to the task.

*

So god weakens me to the point where I lay down my self-sufficiency and my independent being. I let him use me as he sees fit. It is a mighty work I perform now, as I drag myself to the place of worship vis-à-vis the heart of the beleaguered prisoner and mutter the few words that come to me. Not words learned and memorized, not words out of a catechism or a medical textbook but words that come to me. Perhaps not words from my mouth at all but a hand on the forehead of the prisoner, a drop of water to moisten his lips. Suddenly his face opens like a sacred text. He sees, he speaks understandably. Contact has been made. The barrier? What barrier?

Is that the secret then, that we allow god to use us? Are we important after all, when it comes to such rescue operations? Are we, in both truth and matter of fact – indispensable?

* * *

Central to this approach, to 'autism' and 'dementia', has to be the comparative notion of social behaviour as group sponsored, tribe directed and not unique-personal or communal. Society is largely artificial, superficial, prejudicial, more or less consciously legalistic, unspontaneous, ritual, ceremonial, etc. – in other words social directives do not touch on truth but obscure it and frequently contradict and reject it. Needless to say, such a notion of Social and societal influence cannot appeal to 'members of society'. Since adaptation to Society and the ability to survive and get ahead in it are preached by educational and many other institutions, it stands to reason that evidence of truth often has to enter like the proverbial thief in the night if there is going to be any rhyme or reason to humanity on earth.

What I want to consider now is crucial to an understanding of my point of view but perhaps not readily grasped.

To a unique one, sociability and communality present different risks. If we stress the difference, as between society and community – society now sadly as an end in itself rather than as approach to community, and community as open to any and all persons rather than limited to card carriers – then we can predict a logical link, supposedly at certain stages or end-stations in history, that leads on from something like a truth-vacuum to certain socially perceived aberrations such as 'autism' and 'dementia'. In an important sense, therefore, one has to be able to step out of society and into open community, in order to be able to appreciate autism and dementia as other than merely biological. The duality and contradictory nature of 'biological' and 'mental', of carnal and spiritual, is itself modern and societal. The modern psyche cannot be expected to contribute anything of value to an amelioration of symptomatic states that are actually caused by it. End-state society is itself as much of a symptom of psyche as psyche is a prolongation of self-conscious end-state Society. One commenting on the other contributes the stuff of merely popular comedy and tragedy. Evidence of mutual cause and effect must of necessity remain specious.

*

Be open, receptive, loving and affectionate, often listening in silence. Let the unique one find his way to you, by whatever means he or she sees fit, and only work on yourself, either on your unconditional love, if you are capable, or on your willingness to honour this 'different' person.

*

We discarded the term 'autism' as a final description or definition, because it suggests 'self-centred', which usually means selfish, regardless of others. Against this we set our understanding of any human being's need to find his centre, to rediscover, at the earliest time possible in his existence and against all odds if need be, the wholeness of his being and the source of that wholeness. If our environment at this time, when we feel urged to look to improvement towards wholeness, is deficient and dysfunctional, we will naturally ignore it and if in some manner it is being forced upon us we will reject it, even forcefully or perhaps reluctantly. The opportunity we perceive, within ourselves, of wholeness achieved or attended, by effort or by awaiting – this must count for us now, after the manner of human-natural growth, with an emphasis on what is essential.

What sense would it make to call this selfishness?

From the dualistic modern point of view, we cannot help but distinguish between spirit and flesh. We try to value spirit, (only marginally perhaps differentiating between good and bad spirit) and state a preference for generosity, altruism, service and the like over sensuality, greed, vanity etc. Those who are seen to prefer the latter are called selfish. Those who say they value the former are described as capable of sacrifice. Their self-sacrifice shows them to be not selfish.

The dualistic modern ethic is a make-shift thing. We try to make do, mostly in terms of morality but we do not take advantage of goods that lie available within our human nature. In order to do so we have to sideline, for a time, any concentration on externals and internals, namely health and wealth, and look to our inward development, which eventually bears fruit outwardly.

This is one way of imagining the transition from a modern, dualistic attitude, which demands from us a continual balancing of opposites, to the life and liveliness of whole being, which is not self-centred but merciful and magnanimous. Of course there are a million and one ways of describing such a transition, such a change-over from a lesser to a greater good and we do well to take care not to become dogmatic or doctrinal.

This risk and danger of presumptuous opinion and teaching, of insisting upon a universal point of view rather than valuing every unique human being's originally creative and spontaneous contribution to human community earth-wide, is in fact what has to be kept in mind as we look at these two phenomena which have come to be called 'autism' and 'dementia' in our time, (to which might be added all the other mental afflictions like schizophrenia, OCD, etc.) and which are drawn to our attention in so many ways. They are, in fact, drawn to our immediate attention, among our acquaintances, in our families as our own children and grandchildren, as elderly relatives upon whose greater wisdom we had hoped to be able to depend.

As we persist in our enquiry, which in some ways could be described as an essay into the unknown, we are bound to come upon much that is not as it seems and not as it has seemed for a long time. So, for example, we try to come to terms with the world-environment in which the autistic one and the demented one finds him- or herself. Society and community could be called two aspects of that world-environment. What matters now is whether society and community are perceived as closed-in-themselves constructs, at the service of, or even incorporating, modern survival values, such as health and wealth irrespective of any true human-natural being and doing, or whether by society we mean a judicious approach to desired communality and by community we imply an emphasis on love and friendship, companionship, mutual support, compassion and merciful understanding.

In what follows I will write materialistic, self-centred society as Society and community that is set up for some purpose as Community. Every Society is to an extent tribal, competitive to the point of destructive, legalistic if only in the sense of insisting on what 'is done and what is not done', etc. Reward (advancement, prestige) and punishment (rejection, shaming) play a role. Every Community defines itself within similar though narrower limits, insisting upon identity and commonly serving some specific end valued by the members of that Community and not at all necessarily valued by anyone else.

What I mean by society is nothing more than my careful and judicious mingling with unfamiliar others, with a view to making friendly connection with any among them who might be interested in what I understand by human being and humanity, even at the expense of popularity and financial self-regard. In other words, in society I feel myself forward towards the possibility of communal relation, of true communication in a beautiful environment anywhere on earth. It would seem pointless, therefore, to speak of 'a' society, when what I really mean is any intention or occasion of social behaviour towards communality. At the same time it does seem to me to make some sense to speak of 'a' community, though only if I mean mine or yours, or someone else's for that matter, when we wish to indicate something like the present spread of our friendly familiarity and potential communication with those whose existence we value. As members of my own present community, for example, I count several, though by no means all, of my family relations, my friends and acquaintances with whom I am in touch and on whom I can count for friendship and good will, plus – to name but a few – Beethoven, Hölderlin, Paul of Tarsus, Heraclitus of Ephesus, Li Po, Jesus of Nazareth, Henry Miller, Rimbaud, Albert Schweitzer etc., all of whom have at least this one common denominator that I value them in terms of their influence on me through their works. Also, with this definition of a community in mind, plainly all communities overlap with others and isolation is out of the question. In further addition, the notion of universal or world-community, where, presumably, the entire population of the earth – at some given time in the future? – is forever joined in one communality, can only make hypothetical sense, perhaps to anyone who hopes to evolve out of Society into community.

*

We are not hypothetically concerned with sick people in a healthy society but realistically with Society into which those perceived by it as autistic or demented are introduced.

Since Society is modern, perhaps post-modern and of a split personality type, we must expect members of that Society to be divided in themselves, equally whether they are modern members of the medical profession or office workers or housewives.

Those with 'autism' are not members of Society. They are unique in human nature, equipped from birth with potential oneness or wholeness (soul, new body). The overpowering effect of Society on these *blessed* ones causes them to affect what are called symptoms of disorder and disease by members of Society but are in fact a combination of integral reactions (accidental) and responses (intended) to pressures of expectation and demand by a Society with which only psychic intercourse is feasible. (At the very beginning of our study we called this a transfer of symptoms.)

The currency of intercourse in Society is thoughts and emotions, which are psychic. Those with soul-potential are understandably unable to connect usefully with those who have a psyche but no soul. They themselves deal in thought and emotion, for which there are no signs. This lack of signs traditionally disconcerts and angers the psychic individual because it forcibly brings his lack of soul to his attention. He will therefore do his best to accuse the one with soul-potential of illness, disorder and sickness. For the member of Society to remain unassaulted in Society he must denigrate those who do not fit in. In that sense a Society is like a club and unless someone fits the criteria he is excluded, (though of course not necessarily denigrated).

I myself recall very well how it caused me soul-pain to be spoken to by adults when I was a child. The adult might have been one of my parents or grandparents, my sister or one of the shopkeepers who served me. Schoolteachers, friends of my parents all caused me this pain when they saw fit to speak to me. It made no difference whether they scolded or tried to be kind. I cannot recall a single time when I was touched by something someone said to me and there was no pain. My attempts to circumvent that pain were at times pathetic, embarrassing for me, but always ineffective – until I learned to source in myself my own unique voice, and until I learned how to turn that pain, creatively, into works of communication. I must have been close to thirty years old at the time.

Was I 'autistic' until then? It might indeed have been a kind of 'autism', of a potential soul in me announcing itself, shouting for recognition, hoping to be allowed to cooperate in the creation of good work. I could not help sensing my uniqueness and my oneness, my singularity. In those days Society was not yet as insecure as today, at least not where I lived then. It was still much more taken in by its own illusions and delusions. It still swore by them to an extent.

I have no doubt there were others like me, living lives of silent desperation, hoping eventually to be able to surface into an atmosphere that made good sense. Meanwhile one was stuck in a Society that was, simply put, unaware of itself as a meretricious, self-seeking, in turns trivial and arrogant system. Surely some lived in that part of the world too who knew what was going on, had made the necessary adjustment and turned things in their favour. I wonder why I didn't hear of them at the time. Perhaps I just didn't know how to look in the right place. More than likely it was more important for me to be made increasingly aware of my uniqueness.

Why do I even mention all this? To let it be known that I understand what is going on in the potential soul of those who are accused nowadays of autism, of Asperger's, of Schizophrenia. I feel I can understand the sociopath, the psychopath, the so-called terrorist who sees no exit from the hell of Society except by strapping a bomb to his belt. What good does that do me, to understand that? It stops me from condemning and persuades me now and again to touch someone, with a word, a hand on the shoulder, the way I wish I myself had been touched in my youth and early manhood. It stops me from insisting that I am healthy and they are sick, from saying I am normal and they are abnormal. No, I need them as much as they need me, these unique ones, who may appear distorted in their social environment but are gifted human beings placed in our midst so that they and we in community might realize ourselves, leaning on one another.

I know that not all the people I bump into on the street or in a concert hall are fully paid up members of Society. Both in high and in low quarters there are those who have caught on, who don't need to subvert, to revolt and rebel, in order to come to terms with themselves but who have learned how to reflect, to meditate and to love. I know parents who call their little autistic girl a blessing in their lives and a gift from the creator. This is no longer such a rare attitude after all. However it does not mesh with the treatment that is meted out by professionals nor with the attitude of the population at large, who must still plead ignorance, because of a the lack of compassionate, rational insight.

I do not believe I am far wrong when I divide, nowadays, between Society and society, as I set out above. And the number of those who have scuttled their poorly based convictions and are searching in earnest for solid ground is surely growing. On the internet, spiritual teachers abound and they may well help to create a little silence in the midst of the post-modern noise, the insane racket that tries to drown out the very possibility of a little sense. We do still better, however, I feel, if we turn to those unfortunates among us who are typecast, categorized, labelled – and then anxiously ignored because we fear we might catch their disease, their madness, their disorderliness.

*

I take it that **dementia,** specifically now**,** is a dwindling and loss of mentality.

The first thing I ask myself is, how can mind that is well and properly established on truth and beauty be diminished? How is it possible that the results and products of thought should vanish? Is it not rather the case that whenever we arrive at some certainty, doubt vanishes? That when we have learned the truth about something, superstition flies out the window and is seen no more?

Mind is thought. When a man thinks, does he have thoughts? No, not any more than that he has feelings when he feels, for as mind is thought, so is body feeling.

Both body and mind are required for a man to create, and when he creates, his soul or spirit leaps into the breach and co-operates. Mind, body and soul move when a man works. His spirit oversees the work and perhaps it enters into it, if that is the sort of man he is, not afraid to give of his life for his friend. All these, mind, body, soul, spirit are the man in whom his god delights.

He who is rather given to feelings and thoughts, and he bathes these in his psyche, in the mere anxious shadow of his soul while his spirit is capable of neither meekness nor repentance, what is there for him to hope for in this age? When his god now, rather than flinging him off for the lack of substance, continues to present him, near the end of his time when his resistance is at a low ebb, with the true substance of life, will he recognize it? Will he perhaps need a friend, to help him recognize his soul, the soul he has neglected? And given that this man repents of his psyche and accepts his soul renewed, will he put worry, anxiety and brain-wracking aside now in favour of thought; pure, clear, clean thought, unadulterated by the tedious trivia of Society and linked to merciful good spirit, his god?

The ‘autistic’ one we called unique. The ‘demented’ one we now call solitary. His ties with Society, which he himself has not loosened, are being loosened for him, one by one. Shall we tell him why? What he might have done, perhaps should have done, while in the strength of his youth, his merciful god now does for him and all he has to do is know and be grateful. However he cannot know it from within himself, for there all is confusion. He must be told. It must be explained to him. Let a friend put him wise to what has been done, is being done, for him so that he may accept and be grateful, not fearful and still obstructive.

The solitary one needs a true friend. What use to him are members of Society, who are caught up in the very psychosis that is forcibly being removed from him? Yes, we call it psychosis if it relies on psyche in place of soul and refuses to relent when soul-substance is on offer. Soul is god-given but psyche is what we choose for ourselves when we fear merciful spirit and reject the gifts of merciful spirit. We choose psyche for the sake of the signs it promises, the sensation, the excitement, the adrenalin kick, the popularity and renown, the adulation of the crowd.

If you should fear that dementia is setting in, sit you down in a quiet room with a friend who will explain to you what might be going on. If you fear that someone you know might be 'losing his mentality', take him aside and get him to listen to your explanation of what might be going on, and he will listen to you because you have bothered to learn the truth of it. Or if explanation, instruction, enlightenment should seem inappropriate, let it suffice that you offer your compassionate companionship and your cheerful friendship, for they can work wonders. Humanity itself can work wonders.

We are all bound to react differently when we are made to face a surfeit of Social mentality in ourselves. They will call our reactions the symptoms of dementia. They will speak of confusion, of paranoia, of mood fluctuation, irritability, unwillingness to focus on the daily routines. However these are all accidental reactions to our losing what we are better off without. In fact they are symptoms that originate in the one who is committed to Society and they have been transferred to you. Do but accept the passing of what will no longer hold and if you can no longer recognize someone who is speaking to you, perhaps he has in truth always been a stranger.

Both the unique one and the solitary one have very likely not yet recognized the gift of a substantial soul that sets them apart from Society and estranges them from members of Society, who are divided in themselves and possibly addicted to a fluctuating and vicarious thing called psyche. The unique one ('autistic') has no psyche and the solitary one ('demented') is trying to cope with the experience of losing his psyche. Is the unique one liable to suppose he is disadvantaged for the lack of a psyche? No, because in himself he is sound. Will it distress him that he cannot fit in with Society? Again no. What does distress him is that the social world that affects him is not whole. The solitary one may momentarily be distressed because less and less he recognizes himself 'out there' but with a little help he will come to rest within himself.

This is why quite often unique ones and solitary ones are able to savour one another's companionship.

What is crucial, therefore, for both the unique one and the solitary one is true community, which bears the hallmark of such as mercy, graciousness, friendship, longsuffering, intimacy and above all else personal presence here and now. The individuality of the afflicted one may be taken for granted. His personality, on the other hand, resides more in the realm of being than in speaking, doing and behaving. Nothing so much portrays personality of being as a genuine smile. Meanwhile what goes on within is new, profound and precious. It goes on where a sign would betray it, so the afflicted one even guards against signs – and risks being condemned for being stubborn, unmannerly, unfriendly, rude and God knows what else the Social one comes up with when his attentions meet with no signs of recognition and gratitude. And do not mistake an unwillingness in the unique one to respond in kind to wit, irony, sarcasm and satire for an inability or a shortcoming. Where the heart is true, it insists on simple communication; on yes, yes and no, no. As for a supposed 'decline of cognitive function' in the solitary one ('dementia'), why not assume instead that certain things are no longer considered worthy of cognition? [2]

* *

So we have the 'classic autistic disorder', as described, defined, diagnosed, interpreted in great detail nowadays, by modern psychiatrists – but also experienced by loving parents, rela-

---

[2] This business of potential souls being offered to those who seem to us, with our Social prejudgment, strangely unworthy of them – well, perhaps the parable of the evening meal in the gospel of Luke 14:15-24 may shed light on it for some.

tives, carers of the 'afflicted ones', as I shall call them for now; (endowed with potential soul and afflicted by soulless Society).

However let us instead, for a moment, talk about the 'classic modern disorder', the disorder inherent in what is very loosely indeed called normal society, which I call Society. Let us narrow our search down to include those who are generally looked to for setting the standards of this disorderly society, the ones who arrogate to themselves the right and privilege to systematize, categorize, and in the particular lay out for us what we are to think of this and that and how we are to view it in terms of cause and effect. Not that the uniformity of prejudice among them is overwhelming but we can point to a degree of overlap.

As, for example, in the case of the **biological** approach to human being.

Biology is near the top, if not at the top, of modern scholarship. Biologists think in terms of organisms, cells, genes etc. They study connections between these in terms of laws and mechanisms.

We have to be careful here how we imagine this. Are we happy enough, for example, to imagine ourselves as organisms or do we prefer to think of ourselves as beings? Are we human beings, among other beings, and are we perhaps also human organisms among animal organisms, plant organisms, etc.

I have to admit that I see no advantage at all in viewing myself for any period of time at all as an organism, human or otherwise. Not in a million Sundays would it occur to me to consider that nerve stimuli cause me to behave in a certain way, that my brain mechanically influences my health or that my consciousness is a product of the books I read.

According to the materialistic, mechanistic point of view, a whole lot of things are the causes, usually lawful causes, of other things. Just as the fall of Adam (damn that Eve!) has caused us, and still causes us, to go wrong, note our inattention to traffic lights and our lack of genuine care for those around us, so has some Big Bang set the universe in motion and so do certain agents cause birth defects. Genes cause cancer. What caused those faulty genes? Was it perhaps up to seven previous generations' worth of individual and societal nonsense? No, much kinder to blame Eve and the Big Bang.

In other words, from the materialistic point of view, certain guilty agents are selected to explain misfortune, and at the same time one agrees to keep quiet about what explains the misfortune of the agents themselves. Dementia is *caused* by a loss of brain cells. Alzheimer's disease *causes* clumps of protein to form in the brain. Plaques and tangles, *caused* by the disease, in turn *cause* loss of memory. A combination of genetics, lifestyle and environment *causes* Alzheimer's disease itself. In other words, all things and everything is under suspicion. Especially neurodegeneration. And what, exactly, gentlemen, is a disease?

Why are we so desperately out for causes? Why, simply so that we may rid ourselves of the effect – or else bring one about. 'Money is the cause of all evil. Give it all away to the rich.'. 'Money is the cause of happiness. Grab as much as you can.' We shout about wanting to change the world. We want to cause change. Good change of bad change? Don't quibble. As long as things change. In addition, I want the credit for causing it. I am Napoleon Bonaparte. Look at the changes I've caused! I sit on this faraway island and wear my faded uniform inside out and regret not having beheaded Count So-and-so in time, because that particular change would have caused a vast improvement. Take two: Now I'm a bespoke men's tailor in Brooklyn, minding my business, and my son turns into this marvellous writer. How did I cause that? I have no idea.

Here we might reflect on our inward possibilities and on the vast range of good work we might do once we get in touch with our individual human nature – while instead we are bent on causing changes to the world. How crazy is that! It's certainly modern. It may even be post-modern. In either case it's not worth a hill of beans, because unless we opt for human being rather than turning into biological organisms caused in some evolutionary manner by our environment plus genes, we end up with bells and whistles hanging from our hats and coat tails.

'So look here, are you happy with all the evil in the world? Do you not want to make the world a better place?'

Oh dear. Where would you start.

*

Don't expect a scholarly treatise from me. I'm just angry. These neurodevelopmental disorders have been turned into an industry. I wonder sometimes who is mostly to be pitied, the 'autistic', unique one or those around him, who are puzzled no end because they were until now convinced that their own way of communicating was the only possible one. However it is not that simple, is it. My grandson looks at me with a combination of sympathy and merriment in his eyes when I once again sink to the deplorable level of trying to make him do things so as to be able to fit him into my cognitive system. It's as if he were saying: When will you understand that where I am all is well?

'But you'll never get a job.'

'I don't want a job.'

'How will you look after yourself?'

'Why speculate about the future?'

'You don't know what our society is like. You will be punished for not fitting in.'

'I have, as you well you, a very high pain threshold.'

Finally, he is preciously different from me and most of the time I manage to love him. When I forget to love him, I make a fool of myself and am amazed how readily he forgives me for it. He never holds a grudge, at the age of sixteen now. His mother tells him not to comb his hair because he might get beaten up. I laugh about that. Of course she has a point. He understands. Mothers behave like mothers and they are usually right in some way. He is content in his own skin. He lines up two-hundred Pokémon thingies in a beautiful sine-curve under the picture window. Then he reads the full set of Harry Potter volumes through end to end for the umpteenth time. He is patient with us when we attempt to steer him through an A-level practice paper but cannot see for the life of him what possible use all that so-called knowledge can be, when he's sure he gets as much as he needs from those Horrible History books. Then he passes a couple of exams just fine and his Granny gives him ten pounds. He seriously doesn't see the connection but is grateful for the ten pounds.

Now mind you, he doesn't hesitate to state his opinion at times, except to his own mind it's the truth. Strangers, who don't see it that way, need to be corrected, his moral conscience dictates as much. I don't detect any 'original sin', if you know what I mean; he seems to be safe on that score, but he does absorb a few local prejudices and turns them into his own brand of conviction. These days he is liable to be critical of racism, for instance. He had seen a shopkeeper refuse to serve an Indian lady in his shop. Surely that was racist.

'What were the circumstances, dear? Maybe in the past she had made a nuisance of herself in his shop?'

'That shouldn't matter.'

'But aren't you in favour of people from India being treated like local people?'

'He wasn't the least bit accommodating. He was being racist.'

'Did he actually say something like: 'I don't serve Indians?'

'It was his manner. He was definitely racist.'

I get angry. Why is he being so obtuse! But then I think: 'Well, what do I know. Maybe he's right. He obviously doesn't overly depend on outward testimony, on the sort of information that would stand up in court, but then he isn't intending to take that shop keeper to court, so why am I making an issue out of this? Finally I see the light and say: Well, if you say so, yes, he may well have been racist, however he behaved and whatever he said. Let's face it, most of us are a little racist to some extent. So we shake hands on it. Generally during arguments with him it boils down to his way of seeing the world compared to mine, and since he is only sixteen, isn't it up to me to practice a bit of magnanimity, rather than trying to win every argument?

* *

Biology is all the rage. Over sixty branches of biology bear fruit nowadays. All of it bears the stamp of control. Beings, with which one might correspond, are turned into things, i.e. organisms, and controlled. This is a very late-modern pastime and huge amounts of money and energy are invested in it.

Bios – the life that is limited to survival.

Neither autistic nor demented people are interested in survival. However they do live and when we don't aggravate them with our cockamamie modernisms they are good to be with. I find it strangely restful to spend time with my grandson ('Asperger's syndrome'). He doesn't need to be paying especial attention to me. It's just nice to have him around. Also, it's not at all easy to hurt his feelings. He is endlessly forgiving. 'I don't want to look at another Larsen joke today,' I tell him, impatiently. He quietly walks away. Oh dear, I was unkind. I hurt his feelings. So I inquire. I ask him a question and he responds in the friendliest, most rational and patient way. No hurt feelings. No feelings at all, I suspect. Well, isn't that marvellous! No feelings! I could well do without feelings. It's amazing how they get in the way. Much better to feel. You cannot hurt someone's feeling. Think about it. Feelings are selfish, self-centred – autistic? It turns out I'm the one who is autistic, not he. He is a secure human being.

If we have trouble separating feeling from feelings in some sensible way, we will probably have the same difficulty with thought and thoughts. I am appalled when I see someone struggling to cling to thoughts because they suppose this is demanded from them and otherwise they will not be accepted. I feel like saying to them: Go ahead and think. Leave those thoughts alone. In time they will come home, dragging their tails behind them. What are the signs of thought? How can you have evidence of someone feeling?

There are no signs. You cannot have any evidence. So you cannot reward these afflicted ones for thinking like you and you cannot punish them for thinking differently from you. And yet, feeling and thinking are what counts, what gets us ahead, while thoughts and feelings at best get in the way and at worst tempt and betray us. This has to be taken on board, before we can begin even to tolerate, not to mention love, human beings among us, who, because they are human beings, will not be biologically summed up.

Biology – the study of life.

Can the quality of eternal life be studied? Not really. There have always been a few, during the previous two-thousand years, who have lived eternally, which means not *either* internally *or* externally but inwardly *and* outwardly.

Modern man lives internally <u>or</u> externally; privately <u>or</u> publicly. He can become adept at switching quickly, surreptitiously, from one to the other and often, probably most of the time, he doesn't notice himself doing it. This is what it means to be modern. A lot of modern humour is based on that half-conscious duality. When I see modern individuals get together to argue about religion, philosophy, morality and the like, especially in front of an audience, it makes my hair stand on end. Every time somebody wants to shake hands with his right hand, the other fellow extends his left, and vice versa. Like an exercise in silly-buggers. That's because it's all about thoughts and feelings, none of which can be tied down because they are individualistic and therefore absolutely impatient of crossing a personal bridge. Oh, people will agree about what they like or dislike, but that isn't communication, is it. We all agree it's bitter cold today. Along comes this bent old lady in shirt sleeves, barefoot, smiling. Must be a witch. Let's burn her. Or we have all agreed that God wears a hat. Along come theses upstarts and insist He wears a cap. Let's excommunicate them first and then burn them.

Biology, due to our state schooling, becomes ingrained in us. We can no longer see beings, only things, organisms. Luckily beings, in addition to living, coincidentally put a little effort into survival. We wrong them by presuming survival is top of their agenda. We judge them by our mediocre standards. We append modern criteria, biological characteristics. Instead of keeping our eyes open and allowing these beings to persuade us that they live, we insist they merely survive, to bolster our own biological egos. We are so afraid of eternal life!

Yes, that's precisely it – we are, even violently, afraid of living eternally. I'm not quite sure, do we think it means living forever? I fear that the great multitude will never make it, but who wants to belong to the multitude! God's house will be filled, we may take that for granted, even if the highways and byways need to be scoured for eligible participants.[3] Or: First it's the Gentiles that get the nod, because the home crowd didn't cheer the hero. Nowadays you don't even need to be a Christian. Or to be a member of any Religion at all. For some it's enough to be inoculated with this new essence of humanity, which I think of as a potential soul in a soulless environment; or call it a new body and/or a new mind within some totally unprepared constitution, so that the recipient is as confused about it as those who are responsible for him, because what is being highlighted is – once again for, what do I know, maybe the fi-

[3] Christian Bible, Mathew 22:10.

nal time – the shortage of human beings, of beings who have made the effort and taken the trouble to inform themselves of what is at stake, of what is on the way, of what is unavoidable and what is possible – I mean in terms of eternal living on earth.

When I look at the advances just in biology during the previous hundred years, the huge number of branches of interest that are opening up in so many directions, *astrobiology, population biology, neurobiology* – then it strikes me that the nature of the curiosity is not what I would call being-centred; the interest does not convince me that it is careful of the best of which we human beings are capable. Rather it strikes me as a combination of egology (sic) and psychocentricity. However our ego and our psyche – are they not always at loggerheads? Does our ego not forever insist on a total structured control of everything while our psyche needs to dissect, to criticize – to atomize? *Bioinformatics, parasitology, socio-biology***.** Find the building blocks, the common denominators, then let the ego build it up in a thousand new forms and contents. (Am I the only one who is reminded of the Sorcerer's Apprentice?)

No, it's all fine. Surely it's all perfectly fine. Laws are laws and we need to know them. All of them, if possible. Otherwise how can we impose them? It shortens the time, doesn't it. It's not just a case of world-wide OCD. Because if it were a disorder, somebody would end up paying for it and it wouldn't be cheap. I look at the Social population who scour the internet for the latest cures, the latest fashions, the latest fixes, and the great international Pharisee does not keep them waiting. He decides that today we must have this particular thing and tomorrow that same thing is bad for us. He tells us what to eat and what not to eat and when he changes his mind you cannot book him because he is legion. The latest findings are such and such. Keep up! No, sorry, that was all wrong. – *Biophysics, psychobiology, cryobiology.*

I believe modern man's brain function should be placed

under suspicion. I quote: Autism does not clearly present as a unifying mechanism at either the molecular, cellular, or systems level. It may be a few disorders caused by mutations converging on a few common molecular pathways, or perhaps it may be a large set of disorders with diverse mechanisms. It appears to result from developmental factors that affect many or all functional brain systems and it disturbs the timing of brain development more than the final product.

Or then again, maybe the opposite. Let's by all means keep publishing papers and citing each other's findings. Hey, maybe a disease will be named after us!

Is this a runaway train? Are we not in danger of turning into organisms ourselves when we think and talk like this?

I have a friend who takes care of his mother-in-law. She is blissfully happy. He washes her under the shower in the morning, massages her arms and legs, applies cream, dresses her, sets her on the commode, then feeds her a decent breakfast. He sings to her, she joins in, a little, now and then. She chews her food with a full set of her own teeth but does not move much at all under her own volition. She sits, eats, smiles, and – to quote my friend: 'She gives me the opportunity to be more of a human being.'[4] He is seventy-six years old, like myself, and she is ninety one. He leads a very active life. He gardens, paints, burns ceramic pots and figures of all shapes and sizes, he ex-

---

[4] I asked him to expand this a little and he wrote the following: I have taken daily care of Elfriede for many years and we have a unique and happy partnership. In recent years I have been awarded a carers allowance by the State and although I appreciate the financial help, my real reward comes from being in position to continue to look after my charge. Elfriede is now ninety-one years old and although her body is in decline, her spirit is in a happy place and her peaceful, smiling face is a welcome part of my life. When she leaves this world I will miss her. I value her trust in me and the sense of being needed and accepted. I am glad to have the experience of seeing her smile blissfully as she nears the end of her life and this helps me to prepare for my own departure with less anxiety and more acceptance.

hibits his work twice a year. He does all this in a leisurely fashion. His wife retires this year from her work as a nurse. They have children and grandchildren and pets and are cheerfully reluctant to take holidays together because that would mean leaving old Elfriede in a home from where she would surface a fortnight later badly neglected. My friend insists that as far as he is concerned, dementia is not a sickness but a normal stage of life through which some people go and they should not be deprived of it. Sadly, sometimes they are treated in such a way that one can only wish an early death for them.

So let's face it, who has the time, who has the willingness, the knowledge of what is good for him to do and what is a cop-out? Fine. But let's honestly look the facts. Our Society, as we like to call it, is a tragic mess and we, if we are members, cannot really help ourselves, so it seems. The deplorable contradictions abound. The problematic 'elderly' get older, the problematic youngsters get younger.

The characteristic 'triad of autism symptoms': impairments in social interaction, impairments in communication; restricted interests and repetitive behaviour: Now these characteristics appear separately in the wider population of course, don't get this bit wrong, all the way from pathological to hardly noticeable. And who, by the way, is defining 'social interaction' here? Is it perhaps Social interaction that is meant? Very likely. And who has decided on the ingredients of conversation? Are they members of Society, perhaps, who 'converse'? And who feels that this autistic behaviour is restricted? Restricted for whom? Repetitive in whose eyes? Yes, quite right, it is the 'bigger picture' we do well to keep in mind. How do the big pictures of Paul of Tarsus compare from before and after he saw the light? The Pharisee has a big picture alright and he is convinced it is the right one. Then he undergoes a change. He doesn't choose to undergo a change. No, he is changed. It confuses him. Then he buckles down and speaks. Is he mad? Some say Paul is mad. I mean listen to Jesus himself. Who can make sense, nowadays, of that! Albert Schweitzer wrote forty-five pages on The Psychiatric Evaluation of Jesus. (Die Psychiatrische Beurteilung Jesu) Just in case! Don't take my word for it. Nothing wrong with playing devil's advocate.[5]

I must be mad too, because the teachings of Jesus and Paul are essential reading for me. So are the writings of Schweitzer.

Biomechanics, synthetic biology, cognitive biology, biotechnology.

I have to confess that well-adjusted, predictable people, 'normal' people, do, if I am not very careful, bore me to tears. I stand there inwardly weeping and they wonder what's wrong with me. I can barely explain myself. It's because, I explain, you are so well adjusted, so normal.

Well thank you.

What I mean by the modern duality is quite successfully presented by modern man as normal and perfectly adjusted; I am not saying that it is not. On the other hand, I have a friend, a woman, who switches from Bambi to banshee at a moment's notice and her husband swears: 'She's the woman for me.' He explains what he means. The many-faceted personality enriches other lives. The gifted personality has its hands full communicating within modern limitations. You can always be nice to incompetent strangers, they won't mind. What I want is honesty, like the man in the song of that name.

*

I would like to be able to say that there is no such thing as Society, but there is precisely such a thing. It is a mythic thing and it controls us entirely if we're not careful. It controls us by persuading us to assume that all our observations, for example, can be charted according to laws. It controls us by seeming to

---

[5] In the meantime Mr. Dawkins seems to agree with a friend who cannot make up his mind "who is he bigger shit, Plato or St. Paul".

preach independence of the individual, isolation of the person, exclusive externality of facts and events, 'true' the same as 'correct', survival as life – to mention but a few. So when I mention Society I mean the potential for extinction in all of us, however we view ourselves. Without doubt there are those who practically incorporate Society, and seemingly with impunity, and we may be grateful for having the dilemma acted out for our instruction before our eyes. These are the Social specialists, who reap prestige for their seeming inviolability under the hammer of Thor. The archaic element is unmistakable in their activity; and in their flesh.

Against the mythically controlling influence of Society we may set our own personal predilection for substantial thought and feeling, for creative imagination and unconditional love, for justice and mercy. Appreciate it as an uneven contest. Upon sufficient tillage of our field and reaping of harvest we gain the high ground where meekness and mildness become capital virtues for us and we no longer need to resist evil. We gain within us a token of final security. Think of it as the diametric opposite of the Social myth. Elsewhere I have called this token our new body, or a sanctified soul. I dare say you will want to give it a name with which you yourself are comfortable. Then you will no longer seek to quarrel with those who call it what they themselves like to call it. You will listen to them and think: Yes, I know what you mean. Let each and everyone bask in the privilege of his or her own individual poetry. On the periphery, sure, we have no difficulty in agreeing on the difference between an apple and a banana, between a house and a tent. We might not choose to get involved in *quantum biology, in ethology, in nanobiology and evolutionary biology*, but there will not be a shortage of those who do. The benefits are coincidental, tiny and often surprising.

When we study, when we are students, what exactly do we do? Are we involved with the thing we study? Do we realize that we are trying to study a 'thing'? That makes little sense. Then along comes our onset of **dementia** and we wonder what is happening to all our thing-knowledge. We desperately try to remember it and the more we try the more we fail, because, let's face it, initially it was ill-based or unfounded. Why does it fade just now? Because being needs to take over. That is what we should have studied. Never mind now. Pass on or you will turn into a pillar of salt. Value that interval of mere time through which you need to pass, like poor Odysseus through the Strait of Messina. Pay your tribute, which is your acknowledgment of mere time as functional and insensible. Forget that you have a memory, so that you may use it fresh in reality.

The demented one is paralyzed by the prospect of Scylla and Charybdis. Is it any wonder? Look at the movie. However the demented one, by definition, is also Odysseus, destined to get through into the new realm, which is reality. Those who would help the demented one will reassure, comfort, exemplify in those terms. Shall we call it simple faith that is required to get the demented one through? Again, what is required from those who would give aid?

We may not have much notion yet of the eventual extent of 'autism' and 'dementia' across the earth's population. The new reality may well be gainsaid but not held up, not by anyone. If it helps, think of it simply as realty, because what came before did not deserve the name.

*

It is quite wrong to seek a cure for autism. This should be obvious by now. The same goes for dementia. We are not dealing with sickness or illness here, nor with a disorientation but with a configuration of additional events that need to be quantified by every community. We know that a community defines itself in terms of its care and compassion and mercy. These three are so to speak what the members of a given community have in mind and at heart whenever any discussion arises on the topic of a break in communication. Autism and dementia are such breaks in communication wherever and whenever they arise or are chanced upon. Any human community worth its salt will welcome in its midst the apparent cause of any break in communication, or, to put it differently, of any interruption of communion. When something blocks the way – that is the way.

We need to inform ourselves, again and again, that breaks in communication are the very steppingstones to increased community. Spirit of merciful love influences us whether we like it or not. Our own response to that love is what defines our growth in terms of human happiness and personal joy. It is how we imagine this exchange and interchange of love and affection that makes the difference between successful action and futile endeavour. What we do for one another in terms of merciful love determines our relationship with spirit of merciful love – this should be well enough known after two-thousand years of modern experience and experimentation. Any foolishness expressed on that score does not need to be resisted. In fact it barely needs to be noticed, because most of the time such existential helplessness shines through it that true pity is aroused in us. (A friend of mine said to a teenager: If I only knew of God what you know, I wouldn't believe in God either.)

Calling autism and dementia and the like 'breaks in communication', or 'resistance to communion' for that matter, is not such a bad idea, as long as we keep in mind that at first, in the case of such breaks, we are bound to flinch. Then we can remind ourselves every time that this is our guarantee of another genuine invitation by merciful good spirit to improve our lot. Who indeed would not rise to such an opportunity if only he were properly informed! In the interest of such understanding, we nourish any and all community spirit, so that no one should fear he must act alone, must incur any backlash alone or bear total responsibility. Even any anxiety about such solitary bearing of burdens should, please, be noticed as early as possible and dispelled affectionately.

It is the scarcity of true human-natural affection in any communal environment (I do not say Social environment, where such affection is not scarce but absent) that allows so-called afflictions such as autism, dementia, obsessive compulsive disorder, schizophrenia, sociopathy and what all else – to rise to the surface. This is only a reasonable way of looking at it. At my work place, if I am not careful, I hurt myself. The work place of any community is its particular earth environment. No two are the same, as is bound to make good sense. Just as individual human beings stay in touch because they want to benefit from one another, so do communities keep in touch, for the same sort of purpose. Where human-natural affection plays a role in such cases, across all conceivable and actual boundaries of mood, manner and mindfulness, distress will not for long remain unattended.

Perceived afflictions are therefore the attention-seeking devices of merciful good spirit. They are calls for compassionate address. Sometimes we feel compelled to grandstand our intentions, to initiate movements and engage signatories, because we feel impatient to let good spirit do its work. In short, we lose track of where our own efforts may begin and must end, so that creative spirit can do what only it can do. The proper name for such impatience and hastiness would, I suppose, be supererogation. There is no reason why we should wear ourselves out in that direction if we take care to limit ourselves to our human-natural integrity. We are mortal insofar as we are liable to die and we are immortal inasmuch as we may enjoy eternal life. Within those boundaries resides our perfection.

*

Let's take a closer look a that so-called triad of characteristics that are medically thought to come together in autism: **impairments** in social interaction, **impairments** in communication and **restricted interests and repetitive behaviour**. Now ask yourself: What are the main problems, the handicaps, of our society that make us forever wish we could get to the bottom of them, eradicate them and replace them with something better?

Number one, surely, there is the chronic inability of individuals, nations and races to understand one another with a degree of compassion. Even toleration is difficult. If you think chronic is too strong a word look at Israel and Ireland. Go to the internet and listen in on political, religious or philosophical debates, discussions and the like. Leaving aside the inane jibber jabber laid on by the entertainment industry, does it not often seem as if a common language were missing? Look inside homes and see how spouses get along, once the magic has faded. Half the time they talk at cross purposes and have to rush off into separate rooms before they kill each other. Then the parents and their children are at loggerheads. The prospect of an upbringing highlights the same lack of a common denominator, so that ruses have to be invented to try to sidestep yet another nerve-destroying confrontation. Admonition and reproof are avoided in case they displease the child. At school the teachers who can be both honest and effective with pupils are in the minority. The government is never done stigmatizing yesterday's ground rules of state education and coming up yet again with different tricks to service the demand for suitably 'trained' *individuals*. In the not so distant past such trained individuals were required for the administration of the colonies and for the maintenance of the empire. Nowadays they are sought by the industries, so that Great Britain can 'once again be a world leader'. (Why this absurd ambition to lead the world, by the way!)

May we conclude, then, that communication and therefore also social interaction are 'impaired'? As for repetitive behaviour: How many times, during the most recent few millennia, have empires been built, to last forever, only to end in ruins?

Now we have some strangely benighted individuals once again suffering from exactly the same tick. It's not communication, it's not even society, when people agree on murder and mayhem. It's evil, the only thing for which communication is unnecessary. In fact it gets in the way of feelings of savagery and cruelty and thoughts of egocentric world dominion. Did the Nazis under Hitler communicate? Did the communists get together for the sake of mutual understanding? Do the democrats and the republicans in the United States communicate? Or are we looking at different examples of repetitive behaviour everywhere? And don't mention restricted interests. Modern man's interest is survival, the least bothersome survival, the most pleasurable survival, the longest survival! The average citizen watches three hours of television per day. Is that repetitive? He performs much the same mindless routine for much of the main part of every day.

I'm allowed to generalize because I'm angry.

Now when I repeat what I mentioned at the beginning, that our 'autistic' brothers and sisters are pushing our 'triadic' behaviour under our noses and that they are doing it innocently enough, mostly because they cannot help themselves, seeing they are blessed with at least a smidgen of new body and soul, does it make more sense?

Biochemistry, biosemiotics, nanobiology, epigenetic biology..

* *

Being as personal:

I have differentiated between the 'autistic' or unique and peculiarly gifted person and the Social individual.

At present I want to differentiate between persons and individuals. What we expect from a person is communication. The judgement of impaired communicability is mistakenly levied against the autistic one; I prefer to think of that characteristic as a symptom transferred from Society.

What needs to be shown is, that personality is communication not only in terms of standard word-language and various other signs but it works as readily just as being, in the absence of signs. When I am, rather than merely existing, and when I have being – though we do not readily think of it like this – I do automatically communicate this. I communicate being not because I decide to do so (as I may when I choose to speak to you, in whatever kind of language, such as English, music, literature etc.) but I communicate and cannot do otherwise. We have noticed, I dare say, how at a gathering of people it can happen that the one who says nothing but firmly is, draws everyone's attention, while the brilliant socialiser merely tires everyone out, because he is egotistic and therefore not communicating.

It is also worth mentioning that the one who merely exists, absent-mindedly, self-centred, may be readily overlooked, (unless we decide to do him the favour of noticing him so as perhaps to draw him out of himself, encouraging him to communicate, to be personal). What the Swiss psychiatrist Bleuler, who originally coined the word 'Autismus', interpreted as "morbid self-admiration" and "autistic withdrawal of the patient to his fantasies, against which any influence from outside becomes an intolerable disturbance"[6] comes across as the typical bad habit of the professional, when he makes the patient wrong compared to himself being right. The truth of the matter even then may well have been his patient's need to be and to continue to be, (to be gifted, or as one gifted) in spite of the psychiatrist's comparatively alien approach and his unwillingness to interpret the so-called autistic one's being positively, generously and in terms of potential communication.

So neither the egotist, no matter how pseudo-rationally or charismatically he holds forth, nor the merely-existing individual, who neither is nor does, either because it hasn't occurred

---

[6] {Kuhn Robert (2004) *Eugen Bleuler's Concepts of Psychopathology*}

to him or because he is in fact mesmerized by his internality, can be said truly to be, and where there is no being there is certainly no communication.

However – and this is my point – it is enough to be to communicate. There is no need to do anything.

I would further like to differentiate between intentional and non-intentional being. Still nothing is being outwardly done. There is no integration with outward reality in either case. For a mature human being nothing ever stands in the way of intentional being. One may decide to refrain from any and all outward activity while one allows oneself to be inwardly here and now. We may in fact be wise to do this, if we have overextended ourselves outwardly for a time, perhaps at the expense of our bodily spirituality. What interests us presently however is the non-intentional being we come across in a 'unique one', because here it must be up to us to overcome our feeling of confusion and estrangement in the company of such a one *by aiding and abetting his intentionality*. Creatively we overcome our bafflement as we lovingly and affectionately help the one, whose being is unintentional, to be intentional. How do we do this? Why, lovingly and affectionately. Is there a more effective, more powerful way of being creatively? And is there really any doubt about how much good it does *us* to do this?

*

We have a much more accurate indication now of what it means to be 'autistic'. It means to be gifted with the capacity and even with the ability for being, however what is still needed is intentionality. For this, a friend or two are needed.

We find ourselves at the very hub now of the communal reason for the 'autistic one' among us. Shall we say the reason is in order to raise the level of unconditional love and affection in our community? Shall we speak of additional opportunities for communality? Or what about mentioning the general bafflement of the psychiatric profession for nearly a hundred years in the presence of a phenomenon that is bound to highlight the impoverishment, in terms of compassionate understanding, of the very social fabric we seem to value so highly? I suggest that all of these and more are worth considering. Seeing how effectively our impoverishment is being brought to our attention, will we not rise to the occasion and take these 'autistic' and 'demented' ones to our heart?

The case for dementia, of course, still needs to be proved.

*

In the case of **dementia** it is not body but mind that is being gifted. Thinking, conceptualizing, recalling and remembering are at stake. Again we need to make a distinction between the initial giftedness of unintentional mental being and the delay before outward communal intervention. Neglect, protracted neglect, gross neglect by the community during that delay implies that the demented one shouts louder and louder for help – without him- or herself necessarily becoming more distressed within.

This is something we have to take on board. The one who clings to the secret good he has been dealt, is liable to make a great fuss if this gift gets no chance to develop, however since the good he has still does remain uninvested (potential, as we called it earlier) and since he or she is not yet really aware of it as such, it is not very likely that any real distress will register and cause pain, discomfort or anxiety. The demented one who wanders off, for the third time, into the night in her pyjamas and stands for an hour under a bright moon in the graveyard (as an otherwise intelligent acquaintance of ours did not that long ago) behaves more like a sleepwalker than like someone in terror. Asked afterwards what was it like, she said: I have no idea. The members of her family were appalled, frightened, baffled – already the first time it happened. They hadn't the slightest idea of how to respond and rightly suspected that 'things will get worse'. They themselves are the ones whose peace is disturbed, whose acceptance of the status quo is put in question.

She, some times afterwards, almost laughs about what happens. Eventually her family's distress is of course bound to have a negative effect on her and complication (transferred symptoms!) will set in on account of this. What began as an innocent call for a little help with something unfamiliar and seemingly good, becomes distorted, complex and clinically problematic the longer the real state of affairs remains unidentified by those nearby, who would themselves benefit if they but knew.

Why should it not reassure us that the demented one is nowhere near in the distress that she appears to be in? Would it not help us lay aside our apprehension and approach willingly – and above all else strongly? Because what the demented one needs is strength to face up to the new mentality affecting her and calling the old mentality by comparison nonsense and bluff.

At first of course, even along with aid and abetment of the best sort, she will have a go at accepting the new in terms of the old – which is not on. The new mind bears no resemblance whatsoever to the old, principally because it will not be pictured. No longer can we think about thinking, while we think. This, after all, had become quite a bad habit. How fond we had grown at one time of manufacturing concepts, of producing images, of toying with ideas – while we knew we were doing it, so proud were we of ourselves and so taken in by our seeming skills! Did we not at the same see and observe ever so many around us doing just that, revelling in it, garnering applause for it, and honours? They marched on, like supermen and women, into their space capsule that would take them to the stars. We stayed. Something, a foreshadowing of something, gave us pause, a mere presentiment. We could not help noticing how the customary signposts grew dim. Their reflections in the water were wiped by surface ripples caused by the merest of breezes. We were thrown back on ourselves. There was such a thing now as the outside world which had been our world, and being outside now it interests us much less than it ever did because inwardly we are drawn by a substantial presence comparatively so much more real – though unidentifiable in any terms as yet available to us. Do we frantically search for such terms – which will never be available? Hopefully not. Hopefully someone nearby, a friend, will lean in our direction and deplore, with us, our experience of loss, mercifully. If he stands by us, without judging so as not to be judged, how much more readily we will lift up this cross of a mind that seems to betray us – and yet we sense we may well be better off eventually with what is moving into us to take its place.

Then we will no longer look for signs, so as to be able to depend on them for the purpose of salving our psyche. Then we will see clearly and will no longer have to feel our way like a blind man along the surface of things, forever craving approval and at risk of disenchantment and breakdown.

*

Meanwhile **dementia** is described as "a national crisis" (British PM Cameron) affecting 800,000 people in the United Kingdom (2015); it is officially diagnosed as a disease or alternately as a condition mostly caused by Alzheimer's disease which implies a loss of brain cells that is a common cause of disability among the old, also known as senility. Decline in cognitive function and loss of brain cells seem to coincide.

Autism, we recall, is officially not considered a mental illness but a developmental disability composed of brain disorders.

Nonetheless in both cases, of autism and dementia, the brain is involved, here as disordered, there as degenerated.

I merely mention this again in passing. The annoying blight that is spread over our troubles by modern, two-dimensional biology must not be allowed to divert us from our course, as we define both autism and dementia as outwardly recognizable (by us) states of giftedness not yet inwardly known (by the gifted one). We have made some cursory attempt to describe the gift and we have described the 'biological', psyche-attributed symptoms as what happens when the gifted one is not recognized as such but misdiagnosed, neglected and sometimes even abused in the name of supposed cure or improvement.

*

The **transition from modern to contemporary** needs to be looked at, with the view of shedding light on 'autism' and 'dementia'.

Populations that, until recently, have slumbered in archaic dreams interrupted by desultory nightmares look now to the latest and most sophisticated European and American industrialization to help them ignore and bridge the duality that is wrought by the modern, enlightened consciousness.

We ourselves can trace, in our European history, over two-thousand years of 'modernity', which is to say of **flight from human-natural renewal**. Contemporary exceptions during that time abound but are usually limited to individual persons, who show by their works that they have succeeded in transition from modern to contemporary.

The modern flight from human-natural renewal *presents* as a *problematic* duality of character and personality, which is then, equally in modern fashion, bridged in a delusory way. Most of what is still called culture and civilization exists to confirm and underpin modernity. The modern duality of human being needs, time and again, to be bridged anew as the old bridges turn out once again to be delusory. This process of modernization, and the peculiar pride taken in being modern, is often challenged, and is being challenged nowadays too, for example by an increasing number of puzzling so-called disorders and diseases, such as autism- and dementia-related occurrences, including OCD, schizophrenia or bipolar mentality, sociopathy and the like. What we are to learn from such occurrences, however, is not only that unfortunately our modernity is fragile and in dissonance but also that once again, as so many times before during the past two millennia, human-natural renewal is on the cards, especially for those who have the courage to think creatively and to feel compassionately. Our renewed human nature has no need of being modern or fashionable.

The delusion that, for example, the disparity of body and mind can be overcome, or solved, by way of a third thing, a third condition or state of affairs, is what fires the so-called natural sciences, especially biology, which strives to blend a complex of laws with a peculiar field of research. What has to be scuttled, in order make this delusion appear possible for a time, is any consideration, tactful or otherwise, of humanity as the essence of being. As a consequence, human beings are studied, diagnosed, observed etc. alongside all other organisms, as if those who did the observing, the studying and the diagnosing were themselves beings of an entirely different kind or species and endowed with viable outside information. The name for this should be extinct information, because it despairs of all contact with and insight into the spiritual privileges and coeval powers of men, women and children on earth.

It makes good sense therefore that, rather than getting involved, in any shape or form, in the multiplication, categorization and accountancy of the symptoms of modernity (sickness, disease, disorder etc.) we take an abiding interest in the renewal of our own and one another's human nature. So, for example, we may "learn what this means: mercy rather than sacrifice".[7] Rather than wracking our brains over what might be the causes of our misery, or of one another's misery, we may offer an intelligent and compassionate understanding towards the one who is miserable, irrespective of whether we feel he deserves to be miserable or not, considering how he had behaved. Need I mention what this does for our own misery? Or we might look to our own repentant change of heart and mind in the face of what we perceive, rightly or wrongly, as the fault

---

[7] Christian Bible, Hosea 6:6; Mathew 9:13, 12:7.

of the one next to us. We move away from blindly doing what we feel like doing and develop a few creative habits of affection, appreciation and tenderness.

As a consequence, our human nature reveals itself to us. Not only that, but it reveals itself to us as primed for renewal. We notice, as a result of our changed tactics, a readiness in ourselves and in our nature, a potential strength, for precisely the sort of activity and behaviour we have so often in the past admired and envied in others. Our human nature, after all, is not merely a repository of faulty gimmicks and highfalutin ambitions but it increasingly demonstrates truth, light and perfection. These we invest then in our contemporary surroundings and environment. We spend less time worrying about the third or fourth world, about the possible population of the moon, in short, about changing the world, and concern ourselves instead with the welfare of the one we are just then addressing.

It is the renewal of our nature, the transition from modern to contemporary, that is being drawn to our attention in a most specific and pointed manner by these so-called disorders and diseases such as autism, dementia etc.

*

Some of us who live longer nowadays, well into our seventies and eighties, may find that, after all those years of living the modern life of survival, in a society that encourages material welfare rather than all-round wellbeing informed by spiritual awareness, we are reminded by our human nature of its potential for growth. A subtle beginning gradually increases in intensity. What is required is a response, as soon as possible.

Disregarding all other variants in terms of how someone's previous life was lived and how amenable the present attitudes and circumstances of that person happen to be to such a crucial change in inward being, we may call the preferred and predicted state of that person his or her **seniority**. By this we do not now mean a priority by reason of birth, of superior age or office, which would be the more social meaning of the word, but rather a quality of life, even of eternal life, that may not be recognizable as such to the affected person except in a communal setting, such as in the presence of insightful persons who can tell what is going on.

The modern individual knows nothing of this qualitative, final and highest development of the human nature. He cannot help the affected person but will be frightened by the changes that he notices. He may even be angry and scold the person for not paying attention to his modern way of life. The affected one however, the one whose modern mind is fading, secretly feels he needs to do better than he has done and certainly better than most of those around him. He is urged by his human nature to look into it, to consider how he might respond to this call for seniority. Quite often such persons try to trick their modern companions in various ways, so that they will be left in peace to observe and research what is going on within them. At the opposite extreme however, the revulsion experienced by Society in the face of any change at all to the acceptable modern and Social behaviour causes such aggravation to that person's constitution, that solitary survival itself becomes impossible.

What I myself experience as the benefits of *seniority* are first of all new insights into contemporary living, being and doing, and then the ability to proceed in a more peaceful, restful and also playful way. It allows me to continue with my creative work as an author on a new level, so that this present work, for example, brings me into contact with something I have for some time wondered about, which is modern man's implosion, if I may put it that way, in the face of totally unexpected and unfamiliar challenges – not to his survival but on behalf of his neglected human-natural powers and gifts. As a result I find the notion of giftedness especially apt. As organisms we are not gifted, merely mechanical, caused and reactive. However we try to break out of this notion of ourselves as mere organisms and then we recognize the many gifts that guide us, with limitation and supply, on our path of life. So there is no reason why we should not understand and experience the various stages along the way as potentially ready for us, in the sense that we then succeed by investment, response, outlay and such.

The five stages of the new life, as I see them, are infancy, childhood, youth, mature manhood or womanhood and finally seniority. Each of these can be furthered or neglected, nourished or spoiled, harmed or helped along. In all five cases we have our responsibility and at the same time we rely on what is ready available for us, as the shape of what is to come. All five stages make sense within community. In Society however only what is externally visible counts. So it must be up to us to what extent we indulge ourselves in Social enterprises and give in to the anxieties and excitements of a Social way of existing. When accidents begin to happen and illnesses appear on the horizon we may not be ready to view these positively, as wake-up calls and as merciful reminders of a need for change. Eventually we may be asked to leave the stage because a more able actor or actress is required, who will take pains to deliver the goods we ourselves had existed to deliver.

Now we finally intend to name the gift which, at the beginning of this work, we recognized as delivering uniqueness and potential in the case of 'autism'. In the case of biologically diagnosed 'dementia' we call it seniority. It is *potential seniority* that stirs beneath the various disturbances such as fading memory and decreasing attentiveness to surroundings. It becomes actual seniority, productive and exemplary in terms of practical wisdom and mature insight, to the extent that the potential is recognized, expressed and communicated. The good that may accrue to a community from *live seniority* is inestimable. However if we insist on seeing nothing but a morbid judgment levied on us in the form of an elderly senile population, then that is the way we ourselves go. We will continue to fill the death-houses of the so-called homes for the elderly and head there ourselves.

*

It remains for me to find a name for the gift, especially in boys, that is masked by the likes of autism, Asperger's syndrome, etc. I settle on **innocence.** I don't mind using myself here, again, as a test case. Most of my earliest memories begin around the time when I was two years old and being shunted around south-western Germany during the war, along with my slightly older sister, by my mother. We lived nowhere for very long, especially during the last years of the war, when so many people existed in make-shift housing. What will never pass from my mind is my sense, at the time, of 'nothing of this has anything to do with me'. I was conscious of guilt in people around me and vaguely aware of their urgency to punish, which broke out of them violently now and then, so that it stunned me but left me unviolated. Not that I would have wished, or been able, to put a name to the sense of being that sustained me during those times of the utmost difficulty for my mother, whose husband fought in Russia at the time. However even when I reflected on that time during my early manhood, what occurred to me was that during my infancy and early childhood I knew I was innocent. I was alone too, and not understood by anyone, and longing for companionship which never arrived but none of these hurt me sharply – because I knew I was innocent. I know that some religions place original sin-type burdens on children and make them go to confession; happily I was not subjected to any such nonsense. Is it not enough, though, to belong, as a child, to an even slightly dysfunctional family, to feel burdened by guilt transferred from the conscience of others? Ordinarily children absorb this and it does not become problematic for them until puberty or during their early manhood, when they try to link up with someone from the other gender. Now the transferred guilt bubbles up as if from nowhere and causes difficulties. How many tales of woe have we not heard from adults even well into their sixties who still cannot cope with 'what their parents have done to them'! And how many parents, when confronted by the accusations of their offspring, are stunned and cannot imagine what gives rise to them. When we look at 'Society' and see the tit for tat attitude with which children are by and large inoculated from the earliest age, we no longer wonder as to the source of that guilt-and-punishment culture. True forgiveness is rare. Mercy is almost absent. Clemency, at best, gets an airing now and then in a law court. The guilt, that is not even incurred due to wrongdoing, accumulates and acts as a barrier to freedom.

If it happens now that a child is gifted with what I call innocence, how difficult will it not be for him to even speak the same language as the adults around him, to learn the same manners and observe the same cautions before the great standard of collective and half concealed morality! His reactions and responses will not be what is expected of him. His emotion and feeling is bound to appear strange to others, often for no other reason than that with the best of wills he just cannot see the point. I recall a so-called rehabilitation centre for children in Vancouver where I looked for work during my early twenties. The unwillingness, mostly, of children and early teenagers, to react emotionally and to express feelings, and their inability even to understand what was wanted from them by their misguided 'teachers', were interpreted as culpable disorders which had to be operated out of them. So they were teased, badgered, provoked, accused and methodically scolded until they sometimes obliged those who inflicted this treatment on them by producing a theatrical fit of sorts – which was seen then as treatment-success. I could see that these fits caused them great confusion. They were ashamed, exhausted and sometimes nearly unconscious afterwards.

I recall how innocently one youngster sitting beside me looked up at me and said: "You are one of us." And so I was. His parents arrived for a visit that afternoon. His dad said to him: "Well, I'm glad you're finally putting on some beef," meaning that the child was gaining weight. The boy coldly said: "I'm not a cow." That was the end of that conversation.

I felt terrible when I realized I was far too inexperienced to do useful work in such an environment where abject, egotistic adults were paid by misguided parents to 'cure' innocent children. I can vouch for the lasting impression this made on me. A young boy who, as I found out afterwards, had not spoken for a long time, neither to his parents nor to anyone since his arrival at the 'correction centre', accepted my invitation to go for a short walk with me. I had not been informed of that particular symptom of his alleged affliction. We strolled along a path through the woods and he named for me some of the shrubs with ripe berries and some of the flowers. We enjoyed short conversations with lengthy, relaxed silences between. Upon our return to the centre, the leader of the workforce was furious with me. He accused me of interfering with the official program, which amounted to a planned pedagogic attack, over a lengthy period of time, on the child's nervous system, which would eventually cause him to talk. "But he talked to me," I said, in confusion. "We talked about this and that." I don't believe what I said was even heard. I recall thinking: Isn't it marvellous how untouched the child is by what they are doing to him – to a five-year-old boy, who seemed to me quietly to sense that he could not be touched in his personal innocence! He was powerless to alter his circumstances. His parents had given him up. For all I know he ended as a 'psychopath' and took steps to subvert the Society which had 'tried its best' for him.

Since then I myself have not exactly led a life of subservience to the status quo. I have researched the temper of the times and arrived at conclusions based on experience and disciplined thought and feeling. I consider myself to be fortunate, accepted and comfortable in my community and able to do the work I am cut out to do. Around me and within me I am aware of merciful good spirit of love, in action and passion, accepted here, rejected there, recognized or misunderstood.

* * * *

When we feel we need help with someone who behaves oddly, where would we be smart to look for that help? In the light of the foregoing it would seem advisable not to expect too much from the sort of typecasting and labelling for which the medical and psychiatric professions are legally responsible. Once we place a label on someone, we tend to think less originally, less charitably about him. We say to ourselves: Ah well, he is autistic, she is demented, that's that then, we may cope as well as we can. It's another cross for us to bear.

As time goes on, we may expect less fear and more insight in the wider community with respect to these so-called disorders and illnesses. Wisdom, not just biology, is being brought to bear. Those who seem to be afflicted are being accepted as human beings rather than as organisms, while we learn to see ourselves too as perhaps *not yet perfect* and in a position where we stand to gain from our thoughtful companionship with them. There is much to be learned. Primarily however we do well to learn along with others, in a position similar to ours, in our widest possible community.

My suggestion therefore is that only secondarily do we look to the so-called experts and professionals for help, and that we do so with the greatest awareness of what we really are smart to hope for from them – and of what we must not expect from them. No psychologist, psychiatrist or psychotherapist, unless he is a very singular and special human being, will be able to come up with the unconditional, mercifiul love that works so well towards the solution of our problems. Very likely he will be career-minded, he will have to consider his professional standing, his insurance policy and perhaps above all else Society and its law. He is legally bound, along with other clinical experts and professionals, to protect Society against those who do not, can not or simply will not abide by its time-honoured routines, its unexplored traditions, its customs and prejudices. He provides a valuable service. That is all he technically can provide. We wrong him, and of course also ourselves and those who need our unconditional love, if we expect, or even demand, more from him.

The popular way of dealing with those who challenge our traditions is to say they are bad or sick. This allows us to settle back into our unquestioned status quo, to amass weaponry and build walls around us as we slide into extinction. The human way is different. Here we ask ourselves why we feel we are being challenged and we look closely at how exactly we are responding to those challenges. In other words, we reflect, we sense improvement, change for the better. We may not like to be challenged but we have learned that what we like is not always good for us. We may still end by refusing to comply, however we will nonetheless have gained, if only by sharpening our wits and improving our capacity for judgment.

I see it as a beguiling trait of our social consciousness that we suppose we might be perfectible, not as communal human beings but as social individuals and biological organisms – separate, solitary, independent. Ourselves alone. It runs deep in us, this consciousness. No matter how enthusiastically we talk the humanitarian talk, how charismatically we preach the charitable message, still suddenly, in spite of ourselves, we feel yes, surely now we've made it, we have arrived – I have arrived and can finally relax on my laurels. Then we find ourselves hiding under the bed, from demons, or wiping out a village in Baluchistan as reprisal for harm done to our soldiers. Or our politics become the laughing-stock of ordinary men, women and children.

It might also be worth adding here that those who view human beings biologically as organisms usually seem to have only a minimal notion of how flesh and spirit, mind and body, are in truth and reality interrelated and interconnected, so that wherever you touch, the entire being knows about it. Organisms are not like that. They are defined artificially, in a different fashion. Mechanical cause and effect plays a role. The question: What causes this or that? is commonly answered in terms of Newtonian physics, not on the basis of communal usefulness. Upon the dissection of a 'dementia' cadaver, one of the findings is severe atrophy of the brain. A disease called Alzheimer's is involved. This disease affects the brain, which in turn causes memory loss. No wonder! After all, we know by now which bits of the brain are responsible for memory. You can be sure it's not we ourselves. After all we are merely organisms, objects of scientific study and not human beings that may be understood to an extent and loved.

The cause of this disease is still not known. Perhaps the answer, as so often is the case, lies too close at hand for our habitual tele-vision (sic). If we were to spell it 'dys-ease', and would consider how crucial it always seems to be that we remain at ease during whatever we try to accomplish, does that not more or less play the cure into our human-natural hands? (What's the matter with you? Are you sick? Take it easy!) I realize I am toying here with the notion of a cure for all sickness, illness and disease, which would at least demand a look at ease in depth and detail. Also such symptoms as corticobasal degeneration, frontotemporal dementia, vascular dementia and a million and one other problems that cause life insurance to become so expensive nowadays, would become less interesting, over time. So, with a measure of levity, if you don't mind: disease – dys-ease = no ease or the wrong kind of ease. Sickness – seek-ness = too much striving or the wrong kind of striving. Illness – evilness = bad intentions and behaviour in general. For shame! (One of Nietzsche's educational jokes was that every healer should, along with the regular prescription, also administer a portion of disgust for his patient.)

Central to such an attitude is the unwillingness to have someone treat you as though you were an organism. However, more importantly, it is the desire to become responsible for one's own wellbeing, so that one can then be of good use to others again. The notion, for but one example, that one is bound to be just a little unwell before moving on to the next growth stage is not that farfetched. Understanding as much turns that little bit of unwellness into good news, because it signals progress. Not understanding it 'causes' the little bit to turn into a lot.

* * * * *

October 2015)

www.ingramcontent.com/pod-product-compliance
Ingram Content Group UK Ltd.
Pitfield, Milton Keynes, MK11 3LW, UK
UKHW020418250726
13967UKWH00007B/2701